Riddles compiled and edited by
Louis Phillips

Upside Down Graphics by
Beau Gardner

The Upside Down Riddle Book

Lothrop, Lee &
Shepard Books
New York

First Edition
4 5 6 7 8 9 10

Library of Congress Cataloging in Publication Data
Main entry under title:
The Upside down riddle book.

Summary: A collection of riddles with the answers
provided in upside down pictures.
1. Riddles, Juvenile. [1. Riddles]
I. Phillips, Louis. II. Gardner, Beau, ill.
PN6371.5.U6   818′.5402′08   82-73
ISBN 0-688-00931-X   AACR2
ISBN 0-688-00932-8 (lib. bdg.)

For
Janice, Stacey, Mari & Keri
With love

I'm round as a pear,
As deep as a pail;
If you want me to talk,
You must pull my tail.

I work for the church
(I live in the steeple),
And when I'm struck,
I sing to the people.

Round as a penny,
Flat as a chip,
Two pairs of eyes,
And can't see a bit.

What am I?

Next to my cousins,
I'm short and stout,
Red within,
Nail faced out.

If this riddle
You don't understand,
I'll have you know
The answer's at hand.

Sometimes high-top,
Sometimes low,
Many eyes,
Never a nose.
Just one tongue,
Not to mention a sole,
Always under foot,
And so I go.

In marble walls as white as milk,
Lined with skin as soft as silk,
Within a fountain crystal clear,
A golden apple does appear.
No doors for entering this stronghold,
Yet thieves break in and steal the gold.

What am I?

His belly is a boat,
His foot is a paddle,
His throat is a trumpet.
He has wings
But prefers to swim—
Can you guess
A name for him?

What can go up the chimney down,
But can't go up the chimney up?

First you see me in the grass,
Dressed in yellow gay.
Next I'm dressed in dainty white,
And then I fly away.

Riddle me, riddle me
What am I?

He travels a lot,
And wherever he goes
He carries his trunk
At the end of his nose.

I am long and slim,
With only one eye;
Where light is dim
I can have a sharp bite.

But please don't tremble,
For you'll be all right
If you use a thimble
And have keen eyesight.

I'm like an eagle
Strutting in a line:
My beak before,
My eyes behind.

Round as an apple,
Yellow as gold,
With more things in it
Than you're years old.

At Halloween time
You carve me faces,
Put in a candle,
And carry me places.

Little Nancy Etticoat
In a white petticoat
And a red rose;
The longer she stands,
The shorter she grows.

Four legs up
And four legs down,
Soft in the middle
And firm all around.

First say your prayers
And turn out the light.
Slip inside
And I'll hold you all night.

Beau Gardner lives on Long Island
with his wife and three daughters.
A graduate of Pratt Institute,
he is head of his own design studio
and has won many awards for his creative
work on behalf of corporate clients.
His first book for children,
<u>The turn about, look about, think about book,</u>
was published by Lothrop.

Louis Phillips is a widely published poet
who has always been interested in the
relationship of riddles to verse.
"Riddles allow us to look at the world
in a fresh way, as poetry does."

The riddles in this book were chosen for their
language, imagery, and spirit of fun.